# The Water Draft
# Alexandria Peary

SPUYTEN DUYVIL
New York City

© 2019 Alexandria Peary

ISBN 978-1-949966-28-2

Cover image: Gregory Gillespie, Studio Corner, 1983-86, Oil, alkyd, acrylic, graphite, paper, and wood on wood, 96 x 96 ¼ inches ©The Estate of Gregory Gillespie. Collection of the Metropolitan Museum of Art. Courtesy of George Adams Gallery, New York. ©The Metropolitan Museum of Art. Image source: Art Resource, NY

Library of Congress Cataloging-in-Publication Data

Names: Peary, Alexandria, 1970- author.
Title: The water draft / Alexandria Peary.
Description: New York City : Spuyten Duyvil, [2019]
Identifiers: LCCN 2019008409 | ISBN 9781949966282
Classification: LCC PS3616.E266 A6 2019 | DDC 811/.6--dc23
LC record available at https://lccn.loc.gov/2019008409

## Contents

### Water

Excellent Bathers   1
How to Become a Writer in 12 Easy Steps   2
The Gallery   3
Moving Day   4
Found Writing Studio   5
Medieval Contemporary American Poetry   7
"These motorized consorts"   8
Shesangbeyond   10
Redux   12
Swallows   13
Mixed Border   14
Junk Shop   17
The Real Deal   19
Knick Knack   20
The water draft,   21

### Desk

Self-Portrait with Figure in Ski Mask   25
Open Valley   26
Writer's Desk   27
Commissioned Portrait   28
The Runt   30
On the Flap of an Envelope   31
Periodical   32
Writer's Desk as Shrine   33
Paperweight   34
Private Writing Gallery   35
Desk with Cairn   36
Spiritual Evidence for Life on Earth   37

## Water

Paper Dolls   41
A lot of Poems Bathing in a Stream   42
Call Number, Postcard, and Lava from Pompeii   44
Shrine in the Corner   45
Ceiling Poem, Wall Poem   46
Happiest on Earth   48
Bilingualism   50
Instant Transmission of Knowledge   51
Pellet   53
"All over the surface of a poem"   54
Joy, Of, Life   55

## Comma

Table Arrangement   61
Melon   62
The Annunciation, Etc.   63
A Crooked Version   66
Self-Portrait with Brick Red Geraniums   67
On the Carpet   68
Edward Hopper Weekend   70
Venus of Lowell   71
Gusts   72
The Mobile of Family   73
Melancholy of Departure   74
To fill a Gap Insert the Thing that caused it—   76
Lasso Poem   77
Troubled Lawns   78
Deer as Family   81

Notes   83
Acknowledgements   84
Author   87

## Excellent Bathers

In lined water
row after row
in shadowy fluids
on a rainy morning
Excellent Bathers

work makes its home
in a murky afterlife
naked and white elms
stare into a fog grit
Excellent Bathers

fog grit fog grit fog
they speak across water
clatter of four and a ½
stars being added
Excellent Bathers

## How to Become a Writer in 12 Easy Steps

A standard street lamp on my desk lights a bench.
All the buildings on the shelves are quiet and dark
and lean into one another, sleep standing up,
and not a soul comes to sit on the bench the length
of a No. 2 pencil, none of the wind-up toys,
the waving cat, the orange with a hole for sharpening pencils,
not the eraser that says Smart Women Make Changes.

                    Under the green lozenge
from the reading lamp, a steady dotted line is falling
where bats in summer are like a flock of paper cuts
onto this bench, a city bus stop, the slim leather building
in the row of color houses. Late at night, I move the neighborhood
around, putting lovers and spouses next to each other,
the suicides and early deaths together,
ones from Mexico, France, Chile, Germany of the 1980s,
in a new atlas. I sit a nineteenth century poet
beside a modern American I know she'd get along w/
& be the less lonely. I line up teachers and friends.
I take my vitamins: the stain glass window
above a certain staircase, a lozenge, triborough on a key chain.
I turn on *Music from Brainwave Massage Creative Mind System,*
and they sway like water plants on stems,
drifting amniotically.

## The Gallery

A stack of framed poems
leans against a well-lit wall
at the back of a painting,
like a layer of clouds
beneath a skylight,
each of the five poems
in a heavy black frame of emphasis.

It's moving day
into a Dutch kitchen,
into an Italian atelier, under a Mansard roof
brass ladles and copper-bottomed pots,
a cleaned rabbit, scullery basket of potatoes,
a clan of obese clouds.

First thing, I hang the poems in a row
over the pots and pans, over the bloom
of detail, where they act as emphasized clouds
while the melon mentioned in the last
rolls away from a still-life.

## Moving Day

That painting with the stack of framed poems,
the one with the stairs that give you a fright
shown just a bit in the left corner,
stairs that lead up to the bell tower
and a panorama of a great religious city
with gold bells like giant overturned cups,

where the pots hang around
like copper-bottomed clouds
and a pitch black melon waits on a plate
on a table with two legs under a cracked window,

I bring the whole first stanza in and hang it up
in this bare example of a room,
the spider too. Details of the *impasto* soup
waft up in dotted lines, reaching
for the painting in which 1). top poem
is covered with marks of looking
like pieces of packaging tape

2.) bottom poem is translated into
an ultraviolet language, Latin.

## Found Writing Studio

> At TL, two men talked about having just lost jobs. What do I want to do? I'll worry about affording it later. A Busy Day —walk —bank (withdrawal) — CA —A-1 for √— Home—"Borrow" $300 from Lilland Hill -Bank (deposit) -Lunch at Paris C.S. not TL (too much testosterone)— The one unique thing about me I don't want to admit to anyone.—Slash my wrists. Maybe I'm not the only one who feels pointless. I'll guess I'll go back to church Sunday. Home —Starbucks

Found writing about the size of a dorm fridge
is at the back of the poem. The poem is a studio
with one cobalt blue wall in Calibri 11 or Verdana
Narrow bold. The comparison has a faux wood
grain and chills the artist's pear for her lunch
(Bosc pear, as in Hieronymus Bosch).

Whew. Now that I've done the definitions:
No problem. Just made some.
I'm kicking my feet like a kid
in this taped-on director's chair
(other versions included a captain's chair,
Louis Ghost Chair, and a bachelor's seat)

near a laminated latinate, the hot plate,
and a footnote to a Smith Corona typewriter.
Are you planning on telling me where
you found it? the voice on wheels says
off-site, water running, spoon hits a can,
his wheels doubling as green apples or breasts.

The inside of a book jacket, used, bought on
Amazon, of literary criticism on Ashbery.
It looks great near the dot matrix window
and the block quote, those ankle-length curtains
dragging around a breeze from the canal,
a ditch in an earlier draft,

to which the painter's next thought adds
six ducklings as a joke. What did your students
say? By the end, the despair. They thought it cruel
though the book was sold used on Amazon.com.
The words could have been erased (in pencil).
Did he forget them? Or maybe someone

took the book from his shelf at a party or borrowed
& sold it, and it became a lesson in private writing,
the power of voice, internal voice, when not
intending to communicate....you just added another room...
nasturtium, goldfish, a woman with
an oval portrait for a face, a heap of pink suitcases.

## Medieval Contemporary American Poetry

The profile of a stanza, one poem facing another
on a background that's like an enormous banner
the trees worked together to hang up, boulders in stone chairs
in a ring in a centered poem at a left-justified event
in an eponymous field. Is it a colloquium, family gathering,
work place arbitration, coffee date, intervention?
Fig. 1, Figure 2  -stanzas made into figures
of cronies at an outdoor table with the gold pates
of domes behind them a religious city,
the other half some sort of seam that needs to be crossed
as by-waters, byline, bisecting line, a previous line
reflected in reverse in italics in Sanskrit
in Latin in the currents under a footbridge the size of
a staple or the hyphen in the banner 1-800 high green hill.
"Towers to turrets" on the turf of an allegory
a circle of similes, as a flock of floral hands passed around
weave a throne out of asterisk. A lodestar sits
in this mist, with the pinpoint eye of a secret
maternal daughter author.

## "These motorized consorts"

These motorized consorts
walk without moving
talk without speaking
cast black sea pearls

to carp in paper masks
of Jennifer Aniston
to sea monsters in paper masks
of George Clooney

move across the lake
as though riding a Segway,
feet inserted into a static wave
like slippers, dog tags

jangling, matching sets:
Heloise and Abelard
Patroclus and Achilles
Shiva and Parvati

drive around, talking with
one another in the mind
leave bands in their wake
leave strips on the lake

over the unstrung grit
of the water, over tantric
patterns of mosquito larvae
under Rorschach cloudpaper.

These motorized consorts
leave boundaries, borders
crisscrossing the gritty lake
like an Easter basket shredded

that recomposes     into a madras plaid
of pink-green lily pads,
a dozen Christian Louboutin heels
size 7, only the left foot,

leave chalk art of rules, regulations
over rooms of silt, overcast rooms,
leave snake ties and eel cords
from a hundred bathrobes

which are fished out, draped
to dry on the fiduciary shore
where the one who controls
the length of the ride,

the one in charge of rentals,
sits in spaghetti-strap shadows
cast by the axis of a Tilt-a-Whirl planet,
wears a Henry Miller mask.

## Shesangbeyond

she sang beyond the sea
in a 15-second spot
wearing a pink hoodie
with shesangbeyond in glitter
#shesangbeyondthegenius

the sea held between quotation marks
the clouds a sculpture
of large-boned girls
who ride a platform:
dairy maidens and junior goddesses

togas and tousled hair,
B.F.F, wtf? some old guy
in a Panama hat, in a colonial suit
a cockatoo on his shoulder
two navel oranges on the other

is leering at me now
from a balcony high on
one of those beachside hotels
he's writing in a notebook
I just saw a dolphin OMG

like from the tuna fish can
in the pastel waves
of Victoria's Secret Spring
Break Panama City
she sings a song in sequins

the sea was merely the place
by which she walked to sing,
and, in singing, made
the soundtrack, her concert
advertised between infomercials

tickets are at the box office
a shore side of o, o, o
became a track of s sounds
that's what her singing coach
advised her to croon

until she lulled him to sleep
with the sounds of her tween
slumped at the prow
of the recording equipment
her Biggest Fan          a European tourist with T-shirt  SHE SANG

## Redux

fall foliage called bathers and dancers
sprigs of v and y hold up an orange hillside
that billows as a tent, the letters bone-dry
if you take the landscape view _____
_____ if you take the portrait view
_____,

       (a)   ruins of an alphabet
or (b) a reclining giant
of boulders at the edge of
olive trees and grape vines.

in a fall foliage of bathers & dancers
a black vine of notes drops out of an oboe
that causes the circle of trees to spin
and makes drop-down grapes

"           " on the joy, the life,
on an acid-pink phrase, on a tangerine phrase.
In a park for picnickers who kiss,
split-tailed birds are flown like kites:

   (a)   upper rubble
of (b) tv antennae, crosses, spires, wires
penciled-in words or (c) a face of patches,
graffiti of pollen at the base.

## Swallows

swallows connect the dots
connect connect connect
swallows connect the dots

white blue white blue white
der die das il la i le
dots   dots   dots   dots

swallows are roman dots
in the sky over the block
swallows are roman dots

on a hot morning in a month
on a hot month named after
name a month after an emperor

dots   dots   dots   dots
dots   dots   dots        dot
dots   dot   dot   dot

dot   dot   dot   dot
dot   dot   dot   dot
dot   dot   dot   dots

connect connect connect
connect connect connect
the   the   the   the   the

in the sky over the block
swallows are roman dots
in the sky over the block

dot   dot              dot
dot   dot   dot   dots
dot   dot   dot   dot

on a street that served
on a street that served
street that served a dictator

no not one no not one
no not one no not one
not one but two one two

la dolce vita gelato
la dolce vita gelato
la dolce vita gelato

la dolce vita gelato
la dolce vita gelato
la dolce vita gelato

swallows connect the dots
A to Z A to Z Z to A to Z
A to Z A to n[1] to M to z

flags of laundry of flags
garden of antenna garden
to form a letter on the roof

la La LA LA LAX
JFK, O'Hare Turkish Air
LAX, Robert Lax

swallow, connect the dots
swallow and connect swallow
roman dots on the morning

## Mixed Border

1.

A mixed border
of October and AM
of a M-W-F schedule
and irises and
the smattering flat
tery of silk violets,
happy flappy faces
to end-of-life care:
end of the line
as adjective or as noun,
colorless periods
strung together,
now unstoppable:
moves at right angles
around the blank acre.
Like an Etch-a-Sketch
it forms the north side
of an old house, a "connected
farm":  big house, little house
(also called an *ell*)
back house / carriage house
to the livestock barn,
a house that dis
appears when shaken,

[*The following doesn't go away after a few more shakes.*]

two short lines
under the windows,
the eyes of the house:
flower boxes for emphasis [2]

alongside the handicap ramp
and the driveway
paved over for tourists
making a hand rail

and a mail box drawn in
with an actual address
that receives junk mail: [3]
flyers about local gyms,
car sales, above-
ground swimming pools.


2.


A decorative border
of fruit and flowers
from odes from elegy,
of nuts and berries
from the roadside stand,
from the poet's working farm
the not-for-human consumption
beside necessary daily intake,
gourds spray painted gold

[3] then flags and flowers,
pumpkins and pinwheels,
red-apple-for-the-teacher
like a stenciled conversation
from stationary inside the mail box,
as seasons become holidays.
It starts where the farm house left

off, forms garden plots
of Spirograph flowers,
raised vegetable beds,
it draws in the next house lot,
it lives the life it lives,
it heads down a road
which it has made.

   ²        but also a blur in the flower box
            b/c of a few extra *r*'s

## Junk Shop

I live in a Contemporary-style house
which means no Epanaphora, Antistrophe,
Reasoning by Question and Answer,
Hypophora, Catachresis or Paronomasia,
all geometry and glass. A skylight opens.
In the junk shop, behind the display case
Unity, Mass, Coherence (Barrett Wendell)
a mannequin, maiden, mermaid overlapping
and a bald eagle that winks, in its talons
the next sentence as a banner above
a stack of spears and jar of pocket change
or people who answer to "Tribunal."

I will be supplying contemporary detail
rather than timeless points along a line
like birds and water, love and trees.
I wish Felicia Hemans (Mrs.) or William Cullen Bryant
… had done the same. For instance,
who are the people working in the next room?
Could the writer please catalog contents of roll-top desk?
What did the butter knife seem like that day (use a simile)
beside the small faces of strawberries?
What was the red splash on the neighbor's face
when she heard her son wasn't coming home?

To clutter the staircase of air,
a coffee mug silkscreened with Elon Musk
Mont Blanc, Bic, and Papermate pens
a print-out from 10/30/2009 Poets.org
of Moore's "The Fish" taped to the wall
the screen on my I-Pod is asleep
Kiss My Face Honey Calendula
a scarf from a $9 sari at Goodwill

around my neck, Café Bustelo on my tongue, and
I am normally a mouth breather.
I have been sitting on this front stoop
all day / watching myself go by &
"The sea grows old in it."
One daughter is making animals from duct tape:
a ripping sound. Eagle, horse, lion
two-by-two into the display case
where the talon's writhing sentence is kept &
melted lumps of crow-blue and black jade.

## The Real Deal

The statue David by Michelangelo is taking a pizza out of the convection oven in my kitchenette. He wears an apron but not the type showing his crotch sold by venders on the street. He uses pot holders with roosters representing two dueling cities. Stooping under the drop ceiling, frowning, he looks like he's considering which tourist to pick off with his sling shot. Many tourists stand on little bridges or around the dark spot where the priest was burned for having burned others, their books, their mirrors, their commissioned portraits, their fancy chairs. Go big or go home. The dark circle looks like the one my brother-in-law predicted if we used the fire pit on the deck on Labor Day. It's hard to tell whether the statue David is the real deal or a replica, there are so many. He's mine but not mine, I can tell. That ass! Those hands! Those curls! Those eyes! It's hard to live with someone who's always concentrating (here's where I would put a line break if this was not a prose poem) on an attack. (You who are always inside) like the contents of a parenthesis. I've dressed him in a track suit and a gold chain with a cross. Did I kidnap him? Steal him from the museum? Or did he come on his own accord on those thin ankles, walking past The Slaves, the first few blocks in chains, stepping around seismic barking and turd croissant? Even taking out a frozen pizza he looks like he's the lone champion of a smaller, more vulnerable society. It's hard to tell whether he's the real deal or a replica, there are so many.

## Knick Knack

You who are only an Idea
with pastel shoulders
like conversation hearts
without messages,

with swoosh marks
with exclamations
around both knees
knees of patches,

You who get down
on one knee
in a forest of porcelain horses,
who once led me

on a leash of notes
as copies of cold people
watched through pince-nez
and opera glasses

in a display rack of branches,
half your expression
and gold mustache
rubbed away

You who the air
tried to protect with
padding on all sides
during heartshaped

fallingtopieces

You who are fragile

but who broke off my

## The water draft,

lotuses on blotches of water
coins in water, water on water
water about water, at the bottom
are coins to get to the bottom of
pastel sound, words written about water
circular words circular words

dashboard figures in lotus position
patron saints, consorts, goddesses
on the surface of pink     of green
music, reggae and gospel     hip-hop
canals of classical and Latin jazz
though in a water garden, $H_2O$ music

tuning forks of lotus roots dangle
into a pond of piano, rooms of silt,
the rooms at bottom toss up silt
watery Times New Roman font
it starts to rain, rain drops on the surface
circular sentences circular sentences

the pink pianissimo starts up
the green largo, the pond of sound
with "brief brush strokes like commas"
**notes across water**     like black lily pads
dis- and un- in a water garden,
dissonances against the harmony

x x x x x x x x x x
where the lotuses knocked out
the water lilies

words circular words circular
water about written words, sound pastel
water about water, water on water
water of blotches as sound reverses,
passing under the white footbridge
moves to the left, moves to the left,

before banks of irises, before endowed benches
for Monet's beloved Camille, for Satie's girlfriend Suzanne
Valadon, and the lotuses who notarize
Death Certificates, Marriage Certificates,
in mobiles of notes recognize the sound as
*Gymnopédies* and change color like mood rings

In reverse sound, a bright story is told
differently, the notes of happiness put in reverse
walk backwards, across the water
and a non-indigenous emotional species grows on the surface
of sluggish channels of long ā and short ŏ,
millefiori of past and present

I prefer hand-tinted poems

Would you care to have this pond
immediately silk-screened
onto your chest
replacing the Rainbow Brite
Murky Dismal T-Shirt
you're currently wearing
above rows of friendship pins

## Self-Portrait with Figure in Ski Mask

or green V-neck sweater or long-sleeved nightgown
sprinkled with 100 types of local wildflowers

breathed into place. The poles of the canopy bed
pierce the clouds like ribboned castle towers.

In another poem, I look like a man in a night shirt
about to sign something. In this one, a woman in a burka

is smoking in the airport restroom in Istanbul.
She's the new Botticelli "Birth of Venus," the debutant Spring:

100 kinds of wildflowers painted on green skies,
pin flowers, forget-me-nots, on florentine moss.

Meanwhile, down below, clouds move inside
pornographic haunches of draft horses grazing

in a padlock. The local executioner is in his backyard
pinning up laundry—souvenir T-shirts, an A-line dress—adjusting

a cast-iron caldron, boiling things off. I look like
I'm about to sign off or up at the back of a shop, in a walk-in cooler.

A meadow, a lapse in the woods, the oxen stirring.
The bride in Vera Wang tosses bouquet into banners from the county fair.

I move words in gold foil
across a green desk: incognito, duplicates, pseudonym

ambiguities, tubers, a chicken mask
as banners exit the mouths of war horses.

## Open Valley

When the desk grazing in the room
with green floors and steep green walls looks
up, a blaze orange deer, noting a presence, sees
how I am a hunter with a musket—
a Smith Corona in wrap-around alphabet—
lying inside the shadow of the closet door.
A mile off, on the cinder block bookshelf,
books on Pompeii, a dog-eared paperback on saints,
on the ice age, the dark age.

## Writer's Desk

I've taped several views over my desk.
I plan on writing my next book with Post-Its.
A faded Post-It with "Note to Self" and "List"
scribbled represents a good start.
This bulletin board is a cork field with corners of gold.
Maybe too the phrase "In Corners—till a Day."
A rubber chicken, a parody, a horseshoe.
Pair of tickets like tail feathers sticks out
of a museum copy of a gentleman's letter board
with good luck charms, memorabilia,
a talisman—held up by bands of looking.
Also a postcard of / an earlier version of this poem
on a place lined with olive trees & grape vines
with a push-pin as a god's agate eye
doing surveillance. I'll admit to feeling
shock at seeing in the reflection of my pen cap
a doodle in the doorway. It's a reader, looking on
from the indent.

## Commissioned Portrait

> The literary world is a community in that one interchanges
> with others naturally and becomes an insider, not by deals and stealth,
> but by a natural engagement with the ongoing work of other writers,
> editors, and publishers.
> —William Stafford

The gleam from ***
the 25 cent ruby ring on index finger,
a novelty ring (300 calories) given by her niece,
in this portrait of Tiffany the Vth, patron of the arts,
first draws the eye. (Hers are framed in Maybelline
waterproof 24 hour MegaLong antennae.)
In a cluster of opulent words, buggy
Queen Anne's lace is bundled at her throat
above a silk jacket that's an enormous monarch butterfly,
centered and in all caps like a road sign,
as a gold dragonfly pauses on a Blackberry
near the pile of hours donated like florins
& a chapbook under her palm could be a day planner,
one arm resting on the sill of a sentence.

Green shutters revised into balcony curtains
are pulled back by a round of polite applause.
She seems to stop herself from leaning in,
like a friend picking lint off your shoulder.
In the underdrawing, a figure turns to take
something out of the microwave. After a lengthy
French horn and gittern introduction,
a small press publisher stands in the wiry
orchards of the middle distance. Festival t-shirts
this year are orange & come in S and L. Up
and down the olive hill, a low turn-out event,
volunteers are stacking folding chairs.
Now no one's in the window, zoom or full size.

Yet she'd been unwrapping ambiguities from foil
like a gift or food item, shiny/reflective in meta
language, a complicated root system hanging out.
No more talking to the neighbor: she's slipped back
inside the apartment, flipped the epigraph around
like a sign. Got a ton of work to do. You go ahead
and write about what's closest to you. Green shutters
on either side. Window box in a nativity calendar.

## The Runt

Once upon a time, about a decade ago, I came in runner-up in a poetry contest in which every piece that won mentioned excrement—human, dog, bird. My own poem mentioned dog shit on a sidewalk. A poodle that was half a word left an "S" on the curb. Then when I read the judge's book, I noticed that almost every poem included excrement in some form, noun, verb, adjective. It became a game, turning pages and spotting the shit left on a line or hidden in a corner stanza where one might not notice it until too late. This is a true story. I am usually not so truthful inside poems, but nature is calling. When I tell students this story, they all laugh, nervously, a tale of literary contests.

## On the Flap of an Envelope

*My dear friend,*
*we have grown old*
*without one another.*
Figures, accidental

marks on a slope,
pitch tents at a distance
established by white crane
and prepare twig tea.

Each stone once had a face
looking over deep drifts.
Now when the lacquered box
for calligraphy is opened,

*under the brushstrokes of clouds*
on the outside of the lid,
*and the brushstroke clouds*
on the inside of the lid,

a small gold boat
without its rower floats over
the black sound of crickets
toward an empty mountain.

We are made by a bobbing buoy,
bobbing buoy ballpoint,
at a silence established
by the business-sized, or Crane stationary.

## Periodical

A gray-haired woman sits on an attic floor reading
journals and notebooks from a cardboard box
as a dotted line flutters in the air. Drop-down moth

air lift
single sentence
inter-
chapter

signals gray to green, then a speedboat ride over phases
like a bumpy joy ride across town over the rooftops
    :       passing lane in childhood,
graduation veil, a sill of dead flies at a new house,
"shoreline to a thought," intermittent daughter, as it
disappears into the tops of yellow parentheses
where I left the staple in, near a spare title:
Young Woman Looking at a Magazine,
how different the poem if set in a cellar.

## Writer's Desk as Shrine

A mural of thoughts on the ceiling
transitions from pagan to Christian.
… gourds, a brown pear, tubular
vegetables, ugly heritage tomatoes…
in the spring, a figurine opening a window,
a conical flower on the desk that's turned purple.
The fingers of God and a man almost touch.

My desk is from Target. A poster of a pentad.
Taped to the wall: a question made of pollen,
gamma waves, then delta, and roads
made from smoke. The smell of the space heater.
An old coffee can for pens & pencils
like a vase of metallic and wood tulips.
BORN. CALLED BACK.

So what if poems made from profanities
continuously burn as trash in a barrel, a memorial flame
beside a porcelain turnip, beautifully rendered.
A fuzzy orange monster with Velcro foot pads
is dropping brown snakes on the desk
under a picture of Pompeii in a wreath of
Page Up Page Dn End Home.

In the swivel chair, a hunched animal print
makes mirror words. Plus the faux parts.
The holograph of a reader rises like a genie.
Tattoo of fountain pen steps off my spine.
Glassblower, I breathe in / breathe out,
making my temporary vases
on display under the desk.

## Paperweight

These flowers are found only in this poem.
The scent of light, sound of moonlight,
of a small room closing in a blueprint for a dream.
Flowers that will never speak, one-dimensional,
that tremble when notice. The nocturne above the piano fades.
It lingers like a person who is now the door.
Oh, hurry. Hurry before the yellow cloud moves away,
flowers existing only in this poem,
a line of pollen over the grid of my heart
(in a rounded world) (in a nocturnal town).

## Private Writing Gallery

A single-stanza portrait,
a framed freewrite,
xerox of water lilies, the commas colored in,
a close-up of a detail in a poem,
the picture written
entirely with a ballpoint pen
found in a ruined villa,
these are like a list covering a wall
in a poem, shelves of short phrases
at the private writing gallery.

A mosaic woman in a toga
in a Q & A puts quill to her lips,
found in a courtyard with an empty fish pool,
with the voice from the weedy volcano
and a tree that produces for no one
for a thousand years or more
a small, unrecognizable fruit,
the branches and their sub-details

shadows across the wall in the next stanza.
A mural with a deep crack and underlined pond:
a youth is forever diving into the next world.
Inside a glass case with rusty forms of closure,
the sound of my footsteps as I turn away,
a photograph of a decrescendo.
This page left purposefully blank. On loan, elsewhere:
[                              ]

## Desk with Cairn

I've used the tape of your looking
to hold up this poem.
                        Far upper right corner,
spray-on views of a mountain,
100 overlapping vistas    aquamarine baby blue    w/ high, green clouds:
a mobile of lakes
            swings overhead.

The sunflower-yellow back wall
commands attention with the phrase

 "Then consider" the broken-down Mont Blanc pen.
Helped over to the large shade tree of a lamp,
it rests on the stand. A herd of ballpoint pens
is frightened by a prop plane & stampedes
across the savannah of my desk,
bisects coffee rings, dried lake beds,
& escapes into the onyx side of the laptop.
A Composition Notebook. Rainbow made from pipe cleaners.
My payment is enclosed. I prefer to contribute by. [Check one box]

Lagging five seconds behind, a ceramic water buffalo
we found in a vineyard in Tuscany,
pottery dumped to improve the soil.
I prefer a different level of membership.
"The Fish," Marianne Moore, downloaded 10/30/2009.
A 4-winged bird, the shadow of a horse's head,
in a moment from deepest Connecticut.
These notes in Garamond  *interstate is draped like a python*
*in the birches / it's striped w/ take-offs from the airport*

Lower left-hand corner. Like a pile of field stones:
youthereader add the last round sound
                of the poem
coming to a stop.

## Spiritual Evidence for Life on Earth

At the laundromat, I discover my core values
they are like a row of birthstones
Do not seek praise, approval, or sympathy

and stacking memories of a face
on the lid of a machine in the desire for a leader
spiritual, governmental, or romantic

watching the lavender butterfly clock
in its protective cage, from lint corners
boxes of detergent for $1.25

Do not seek approval from a vending machine
certainly not a woman roller-skating down a rainbow
that's emerged from her forehead

the manager looks like a Tasmanian Devil
clothed from the Lost & Found and says a bullet
came through her wall, infected & took her husband

The pastel words *praise* and *sympathy* on my finger
before returning to the mote I live in
a tiny apartment with fold-away rooms

a guy named Peter or James wheels in a bicycle painted black
got Mary(Jane) in his jean jacket pocket
consults the manager for love advice like an oracle

The leather jacket I'm wearing doesn't look good on me,
the artist boyfriend on the cell phone will nev' commit
and two skanks have my wet laundry in their basket

I should be watching the words I use
people are meditating in the Shambhala
tradition at the U-U across the street,

leaky sandwiches are selling at Orange Duck,
at White Castle, the tavern of sawdust on Canal Street
near a Guatemalan restaurant, near a Colombian restaurant

that's trying not to jeer at the chain Margarita's,
the shiny Dunkin' Donuts was erected on the exact
spot as the other Dunkin' Donuts, now that's what I call spring cleaning,

a few blocks from the unused cathedral, from the fortress
of BAE, a buttress unfolds like a giant pincher
as I walk home, basket of damp shrouds

→ swaddling clothes on my hip,
careful to step around the reverse sunset in
puddles that sound like piano, like Erik Satie.

## Paper Dolls

Still life holding a self-portrait in a landscape.
Self-portrait posing in a landscape with still life.
Landscape with a still life that models as a portrait.

Which self-portrait cradles a green Lazy Boy recliner
in front of a FULL parking garage, a house built
from a kit, with a car fueled on French fry oil?

\*\*\*\*\*\*\*\*\*\*\*\*\*\*\*\*\*\*\*\*\*\*\*\*\*\*\*\*\*\*\*\*\*\*\*\*\*\*\*\*
Um, oh, like, ah, like. Um, oh, like, ah, like.
In the daisy chain, with paper dolls, after multiple tabs

of multi mountains tipped in acceptance green
lightning illuminating greenly a pocket,
bonfire in the background, mowing in the foreground.

3 more hold up the next 3 like waiters with platters,
like trees with tiny trees grafted onto their trunks
or words with smaller exponential words—

\*\*\*\*\*\*\*\*\*\*\*\*\*\*\*\*\*\*\*\*\*\*\*\*\*\*\*\*\*\*\*\*\*\*\*\*\*\*\*\*
Um, oh, like, ah, like. Um, oh, like, ah, like.
# of people-shaped landscapes > than still life or portraits.

Rock, paper, scissors: they drop into place
and mill around or start hiking groups,
the tan angel, Judith who made the news, the rookie

from the auction house, holding Polaroids of loved ones
propped in bowls of fruit, "Wet Nurse in Landscape
Visited by Officials" or a Sears painting that turns

out to be a Caravaggio, worth billions,
of a unicorn beside raised ranch, near a waterfall,
knitted asterisks gushing over the reverse couch.

# A Lot of Poems Bathing in A Stream

Bathers beside the stream
B. In the stream
Poems Bathing in the Stream
who read about people before the stream,
behind the stream, after the stream's
been given an eloquent introduction

are not quite the same as people
who read *People Magazine,*
pantheon of Hollywood and runway,
in a steamy bath, the vapors
twine between lily pads.
Minnows are comparisons in the shadows
to, for, with the stream,
in splashed eloquence

where birds hang announcements
from an intercom. No doubt
poems bathe in the stream,
giant spheres of spirit & action,
grown men & women with sonnet parts
that look like wheels turning in their faces
and may need an oil change,

who splash each other & delay certain splashes,
among stalks among asterisks,
people who head back to homes
that really don't stand still, like the twirl
of what's been said in the water. That's how

it happens, or may have happened, until
the marble bust of the life guard
blows Thine whistle: someone has waded too far out
in the ¾ cup shallows of the writer's voice.

Meanwhile the epigraph shifts location,
like a heron who's decided to not trust us,
a few yards off in the single-spaced water…

## Call Number, Postcard, and Lava from Pompeii

An arrow-shaped poem rests on my desk in the year-long room
the arrow dries its wings like an insect
the arrow moves its airmail mouth
How it traveled underground on an overcast sky
saw a young tree lifting its root ball
like a suitcase          over speed bumps of contrail
How it was like a room in the sky
with windows at ground level
a view of the shuffling clogs of pilgrims
How it landed in the cumulous up-do
of a giant woman who looked good wearing it
though she was unconscious of the arrow
with looks more Virginia Woolf than Clarice Lispector
Oh yeah? I yank out the day-glo yellow microphone
that I've let grow the whole time
in the courtyard upholstered in Midnight Green.

## Shrine in the Corner

A reader's interpretation is set on a shelf
as a small unframed canvas
among jars and white canisters,
an espresso pot and a wine bottle,
a plastic baggie of red peppercorns.

It looks like an eye test    pink, yellow, blue
circles connected by lines
This is just a test. A test given to pronouns
of the emergency broadcasting system.
-the way a frog or cat sees.
A process or cycle rather than list or hierarchy.

This still life of a page includes
a stenciled bowl of fruit,
a paint-by-number of a minute ago
near a window that will never offer a view,
set on several lines of fake brick wall,
several lines in which "brick" is used.

## Ceiling Poem, Wall Poem

A poem on the ceiling
takes a wild horse half-drawn

in Calibri on a Post-It,
a stick figure pursuing

a wish with an arrow
in a text message

about cave art.
Overall, put more joy

on my face, in my body,
look up, keep looking ↑

that's the banner flown
in a stanza as the wave

of my tongue rests
behind the Stonehenge

of my teeth. Taped to
the yellow kitchen wall

is a brochure on how to look up
more often than down

into sunflower lemon.

\*

Poems can be diptychs, triptychs,
brochures, folded three ways,
a poster session upright
on a green table with memorabilia
and *memento mori*, odd roots
and tubers, driftwood wigs.
Take this one, for instance,
two sections with a list like ivy
running up a wall: it's displayed
among Polaroids of holidays,
an enormous chin on a moon
nailed to kitchen wall otherwise
covered in chicken masks.
On one side, a blank for a madonna,
on the other a ping-pong ball
with a face painted on it,
an asterisk keeping them apart.

## Happiest on Earth

*for M, S, and S*

That red deer dancing in circles
leaping after a red flag
the bandana of its tail
at twilight next to grape fields

as though dialing up the earth
the doe multiplies herself
into a carousel of dancers
hyphenated, holding hands

every few seconds jumping high
a grand jeté in a nursery rhyme
the chandelier in the sky sparkles
until we four cross diagonally

over rows 44, 43, 9, and 7
and are watched by a pagan
in the vine-covered walls.
That lady quiet in a blue shrine

with beads, plastic flowers
and a battery-operated candle
a spider stitching her cheek
transmitting a lullaby plainsong

she who briefly protects even us
outsiders at a field cemetery
of four names, village of
wine and oil, oil and bread

the electronics in the sky flicker
on every grave, a photograph
Nova, nova. *Veni, veni*
as we proceed latitudinally

in olive trees and rake the land
to the empty monastery
with an open well, straight shot
to the 12th century, to pitch

darkness, to putting this fair face to
the most (which one) frightening
moment on earth.

## Bilingualism

I saw my grandmother on a billboard
stretched out in a green dress like a snake
out on a walk alone in swamp maples.
Reclining, smoking a cigarette as though
in an advertisement for bourbon in a casino,
watching me and never intending to speak.
Not a single wood chip of a word,
would not give up a single playing card of a leaf.
All I could think was, Who was she
to sell anything to, her poles rusty
in that expanse of reeds and skunk cabbage,
with a weasel animal that slipped into the shallows...?
Replaced in a week by an ad for a local optometrist.
That was the one time I saw my grandmother.
Such was the first and last time I saw my grandmother.

## Instant Transmission of Knowledge

In 1982,
Wolf Man Jack
counted down "greatest hits"
from 40, 40 Solid Gold
puddles at the Top of the Charts
from the alarm-clock radio,
the sound of the dryer shuffling
for Saturday laundry
while wolf spiders
rode on the top of my head
though no one told me
as I went to my *Psycho* shower scene,
a pre-teen.

In Amherst, MASS,
I had a pet leaf
called Called Back
that followed me everywhere
a red asterisk on October sky
The angora bush
of loneliness stood on the porch
of the apartment complex
ringing the doorbell,
the fraternity next door got a keg.
L'Oréal Paris 6R, Light Auburn, Warmer
Revlon 56, Brilliant Bordeaux but Brown
Emily Dickinson had auburn hair
apparently or strawberry blonde
like an oak leaf
apart from its tree.

Leaning back against the railing
on the unpainted deck
the merlot has gone to my head
while someone grills eggplant
and we talk about whether evil
exists or if it's a type of social interaction,
the gray climbs upward
into Minerva, Pamela,
Reverend 2013 (Called)
of First Parish U-U
in Scituate, MASS,
who has gone gray,
unpainted pole the gray climbs upward

## Pellet

Near the written sound
the dripping of trees
and the reverse sunset

a mostly mauve and orange
or a yellow and black
or scarlet-yellow zig

native pattern with caribou
turns morning-glory blue
a hand painted sunrise

I wear on a leather cord
around my neck, pellet
of just a few syllables

capsule of landscape
Bead-Sized Landscape
swinging from my throat

while polar stars of faith
in my ears zip in
opposite directions

## "All over the surface of a poem"

All over the surface of a poem
circled parts from 1906
I looked at for 10 minutes in 1989
at 2025 Benjamin Franklin Pkwy
with a first boyfriend I didn't stay with
-though his namesakes have haunted me since-

every other line the opaque goat,
the vase woman w/ a vine of notes,
a ring of dancers (in 4 spots).
The stanza is descrip- , is decor,
-tive, -ated like a footlocker

w/ 26 scratch 'n sniff parenthesis
(wild strawberries discovered in the grass),
      -splashes of trees,
No. of times I've visited this page.
The three drawers of the poem
(1)  hold maps from stories,

(2)  a Pop Art composition notebook &
(3)  the screensaver, coffee mug, mouse pad, calendar.

## Joy, Of, Life


I pick up the splashes
                  that leap up around words
in bumblebee black & yellow
                              shock wave suits.

I lift splashes
                  and hold them for 5-10 seconds
like sunrises tucked
                            behind place holders of hills

because I'm searching
for the lake with a handle.

A grove starts to spin
                        as a ring of dancers,
triggered by something
I said
                  (maybe that I'm "searching"),
& pulls up references

to "splash"
                in a clearing.

                        *


In a clearing,   *splashes of paint,*

*splashed with fear*

*he splashed wine on her white dress…*

and this variant:

*I'm flattered and honored.*

        *The woods is a complicated splatter of emotion*

look like splashes of writing,

        foliage phrases

in mascot colors
        blue and web orange,

a version of Matisse's "Joy of Life"

except the dancers, musicians &
        screensaver picnickers
who recline to kiss
are in storage,

(a copy of the painting lies several lines below)
(between earlier versions of this poem)

the circled parts—
    musician performing for goats,
     lute player on mute
figure with a vine of notes—

now a dried sea bed

where only 20 minutes before
the lake w/ a handle had been last spotted.

like contact paper in a drawer,     *like an apple orchard covered in white-out*

—with or without permission     from the Barnes Foundation of Philadelphia.

the sounds of a ping pong tournament     from below. In the cargo hold,

the river of profanity from an earlier version,     ½ ton compressed poems,

crates with an evil eye on the outside,     the passing thought, Watch out for
those trees;

they're what changes everything,     the repeated element that shifts the scenes,

and the real ending of this poem     like a false eye on a tail to fool predators,

if I get down on my hands & knees,     I see at the bottom, a scarlet lake

with its curvature of light.

\* texted stanza
\*\* a poem written on the ceiling
\*\*\* a cave painting about the fine arts

*

In the woods of written sound
the ping, the dot a dot dot
schwump schwump schwump
spack a speck speck:
ahem, splash, splut-whoosh. Vroom:
1. sound of a fast-moving car
2. also the title of a Roy Lichtenstein painting.
& ha!
1. (laughter): not boisterous
               but amused
2. an exclamation used by the good guy
jumping out of bushes to surprise a villain.
-I need to turn back.

*

On the shore, words arch their backs
                       as $1 Fortune Fish
& puddles are they that flee me
            up bases of trees
studded with butterflies.

Next, I crawl to the edge of a pond

            & step inside the surprised water

 and pull it on.


I zip the suit all the way to my chin,

        zip up and up

amid the peeling trees...

Floating at the bottom

        are more words

like petals in a Dixie cup

        like table decorations at a wedding.

I let myself drift
down one dimensionally
                like a sheet of paper
                until I am lying on top
                like one leaf joining another leaf
at the bottom of a river.

## Table Arrangement

Salt cellar, pepper mill,
parking garage, the Coliseum,
Pantheon, Leaning Tower
of Pisa, a lighthouse from Maine,
tableside, on a green table cloth
2 over, 1 across.

At the long table, the 12 Marvels,
Field of Miracles, bottle of
suggested wine, a shopping mall
and the Roman Baths
stateside, on a red checkered table
3 over, 1 down.

Way across the room,
a couple spooning food into a baby
as the waitress arranges a farmhouse,
marble quarry, the Acropolis
on a placemat of Pompeii. Switching tables
is like skipping a soul across water,
like finding the 5-letter word for.

Who's seated himself one table over
but the love of your life
barely disguised as a lonely tourist,
the scholar who smelled of farts,
the bookstore owner who lived over a labyrinth,
or an old local still in his overcoat
hunched over a bowl of soup?

## Melon

As if it rolled free of an ellipsis:
one of the round clouds on the horizon
from the sky at the back of a short story
or from a stack of fragments in the atmosphere,

the melon that left the poem,
vacated the painting. It reappears
for a few minutes in a drowsy town when
a woman visiting her pregnant sister
brings fruit for their coffee.

The melon gashes
the bottom of the paper sack,
rolls down the palisade, down the arcade,
the colonnade, through triumphant arches,
past frescos of lions, grapes, men,
past the bored goddesses holding up
tilting pitchers of water turned to stone.

It rolls into an empty city park
on a cloudless October day
and comes to a full stop
at the statue of a general on horseback,
cannon balls gathered like children.

# The Annunciation Etc.

I.

In a triptych of
The Annunciation, Journey To the Manger,
Shuttle To-From Airport,
the closet with fold-away
ironing board and suitcase stand,
a valley in the lobby
of daffodils where a continental breakfast
is provided starting at 7 AM,
at least no bed bugs, not a meth lab, this Motel 8
Red Roof, inn at day's end.

She leans in closely:
angel with piercings & a sleeve tattoo
of bird wingtips, tear-drop
inked onto a cheekbone.
In Sweden there are a lot of single mothers.
We need to counteract the low birth-rate
of this nation, an aging community
also in Italy,

a red bean in a drawer
of the nightstand
rolls around.
Which one of these words will do the deed?
She scans the scroll emitted by the lily
is pollinated by a gold-leaf word.

II.

Just looking for a place to sit down
even a bucket seat at a fast-food restaurant.

They pass the bloated figures
of Fernando Botero, a loitering

Ronald McDonald posed
as Michelangelo's "David,"

gondolier in striped shirt
who leans on his pole, cell phone to ear,

gladiator in flimsy loin cloth,
sword propped against a carry-on,

smoking an e-cigarette.
The man in the polo shirt

is scowling & leads a mastiff,
the woman pregnant & frowning

in a neon Armani shift dress
trails behind through Chanel, Dior,

through duty free leather goods
Venetian glass squid-ink pasta

red checked cloth suggested wine
through an overlapping crowd of duplicates

with gold halos all the way to the archway
the Bridge of Sighs, the Spanish Steps,

may or may not be angels with electric candles.

III.

Crisp folds in the blue background
of paying-for-college, sheets and pillow.
The baby is born and passed to two weeping men.
Madonna in a johnny, daffodil in a glass beside the bed.
The father who works for Wal-Mart holds
the hand of his daughter, raises her alone.

## A Crooked Version

Three cantaloupe separated by commas
In the market stall. A house dress
On the hook by the door. Potholder
Shaped like a rooster never crows.
The bread uses no salt because of a feud
Commemorated by a striped pole kept near a pew.
The crack in the plaster looks like a knight
In far-off, black-&-white tiled fields
With ditches like gutters at a bowling alley.
In the insurance calendar for 1956 over
The stove, a picture of a family of seven,
A family of fruit gone to stone.

# Self-Portrait with Brick Red Geraniums

The ballpoint animal of a signature appears in the lower right hand corner of a poem. It emerges from this gold corner after a landscape of mildew and a windowless contract that opens onto the poem. The signature heads to the mentioned desk to tussle with a flock of *–ly* words on the blotter before reaching the bright light of a blog. I watch its progress from my small chiaroscuro square of a room at the back of a merchant's shop where I look like a man about to sign for something, a minister or statesman in a frilly shirt, holding a quill. In a frame in another stanza, near unsigned street voices, a cockroach moves over the sink, headed to words on a shelf for sugar, espresso, wine, oil above a kitchen table of white geraniums.

## On the Carpet

Squeeze toys and pack animals, sentinels, the emissary,
a militant, five-member jury, the consulate, prodigal prodigy,
Roberto Bolaño, Hummels, a tenure committee, Robert Lax,
Alfred Starr Hamilton, & Mrs. Felicia Hemans dolls
hold poses on the third floor of the Dream House
when afternoon is spilled like laundry detergent on

the Berber carpet in front of the TV. The story acted out
is about falling in love with the wrong person, eating a bad meal,
being discovered for treachery, told to move on, about tickets
emerging from a rain cloud. Trailer Park, a larger available model
of the Studio of Inner Life, a Pleasure Boat, the Vatican, a Viking ship,
the White House with a hole for sharpening pencils

on the carpet sprinkled with school-bus crystals, lying-in-front-of-the-TV
-watching-daytime-drama powder. Whenever I walk on a landfill
& the toys and steering wheels of my past jangle underneath,
whenever my hand brushes a tray at a flea market, or my left side
knocks into a shelf at Goodwill, the *latissimus dorsi* & its antagonist
muscle groups *deltoid* & *trapezius semispinalis dorsi* in direct conflict,

a commotion is caused in Aisle 5, & I come across my bath kitty,
red paint still on her mouth. She clutches a ball, a pineapple
or a grenade, that far-away look in her eyes.
… A burglary of life has happened. Two Pekingese squeeze toys
are stationed outside the Secret City, are cute are blonde carry hockey sticks,
have earnest brown eyes & a mole, are wearing Calvin Klein underwear.

From the cracked-open pleasure boat a shadowy sentence streams
along with the contents of the boat…a chair made entirely from chance,
a table shaped by weather, tiny pieces of a mahjongg game like rodent teeth.
Called to the carpet, I approach as spittle; I gestate. I am in talks with rabies.
I conceive myself. I howl. I am blocked by arm-sticks. I gesture
with personality, a downturn in expectation, they levitate with translation

because I am "in talks with rabies." I change my expression from malice to apprehension to condescension (a baby blue & pink aurora borealis switches on). A vanilla scent comes from holes in their rear ends.

## Edward Hopper Weekend

      In my Edward Hopper weekend,
apartments which could be empty office spaces
in blocks of buildings that come with last names.
Cheap rent, lots of space, and a golden dust
from isolation I prefer to call solitude,
every phrase like a tinted bank of clouds
presiding over a landscape, a herd of trees.
In a green camisole, I perch incongruously
on the edge of a desk and finger a paperclip,
perverse happiness at scarcity, only a lunch left
behind in a brown bag in the vintage office fridge,
while looking out at the early morning
factory town, the way the light hits the brick mills
that rise like a row of castles along a golden Rhine.

## Venus of Lowell

A bust of Venus in a shop window
sits in the kind of light from after
the holidays, early Sunday morning
winter in a mill town. Her neighbors
—a shoe repair shop, pawn shop,
sun-faded photos of jets taking off
in the travel agency, combs in
disinfectant in a still life with hair dryer
and tinsel.

Lady Love, bare shoulders,
white stone curls, is unmoved
by the introduction of a shoe horn.
Hers is a view of the bus stop, usually
passengers out for a quick smoke,
backs to the wind, today, no one.
Bees return to reclaim the honey
in the baklava, a few squares
on wax paper. By Tuesday,

Venus is wearing a men's green V-neck
sweater, a bare-chested mannequin
set across from her. As a jade plant
in a display of fichus or as the library vine
from a Christian Science Reading Room
or lucky bamboo amid peace lilies,
I am happy for her and raise up
a helium balloon though my tinsel
already glints.

# Gusts

The unmarried daughter turns to speak to her parents,
                                                     adjusting her fruit & flower hat
as the green doors on the Catholic church close,
                               a thawing day, in the chasm
between winter and spring,            zero men in coveralls lean in doorways
       on warehouse street, at the bowling alley,
                                       petrol station, shoe repair shop.
The dams, water half-frozen, are a mouth open to form
                                         a lion's yawning,
frozen speech over the beast's tongue,
                           an Etruscan lion
in a mill town ending in –ester
                           named after a Roman encampment,
i.e.: Manchester, Winchester, Worcester, Bicester, Dorchester,
                           Rochester, Chichester, Gloucester, Leicester.
(On the same point along a line
                 fifty-six years later, in restored mills,
downward dog and lion's pose
                 the day's putrid speech unspoken anger gushes
as syllables, syllables, syllables as
                 I bend over deep ditches,
canyons, gorge of interpersonal ice.)
In the afternoon,
                 three bean salad and deviled eggs,
a few hours listening to the radio,
                               newspaper shop, vacuum repair,
pastry from Gus the Greek's, charity offices,
                         stiff laundry lines
where the triple deckers lean into one another.

## The Mobile of Family

                turns slowly on a Sunday
over the Lazy Boy
and the Lazy Susan.

        -primary thoughts and feelings
      are blotches and splashes
connected by travel-
                            Swish marks
      indicate the family is mobile.

A pinstriped in-law
        with a morning glory in his buttonhole

moves to the right—
that yellow blob is Lil Sis
above the fichus plant,

so far out on her black italicized line
                            at least she always comes back.

"Hey, Tony!" a feather-shaped punk shouts. He hates those jokes.
At least we're all connected now

over the photo album on the coffee table
and tray of pine & vanilla diamond cookies

a breeze turns us to the stadium in the dead tv

        the cobalt I, the steel you

"No doubt we're better off
this way"

oh chandelier of ancestors
oh stuttering ceiling fan

## Melancholy of Departure

I'm so lonely in this place
even the tug boat and train are on a date.

Everything's on a date,
even the vehicles meant to take me away from this place.

I'm lonely because I'm a traveler
always headed someplace new.

I don't feel excited about traveling
or heading anywhere so new and blank.

Perhaps I'm leaving someone behind,
my boat has to be that one, The Melancholy of Departure II.

What is this pile of zigzags?
High copper walls, the speech of trains,

pastoral pollution, II., too.
The train departs platform 2, beside the bananas, *binario due*:

the moping figure, red tower,
clock bleeding silver on the half hour,

now a moped figure
in the absence of thought, of silence in the afternoon,

waited twenty years to say it, too,
poles in the water, a duet,

the common pastry nailed to a wall,
statue wearing glasses of asphalt,

the fact that nothing will ever
happen, not for a poem, not this one.

## To fill a Gap Insert the Thing that caused it—

Peggy loved art: Marcel Duchamp, Max Ernst, Samuel Beckett, Yves Tanguy
foursome threesome, though never Jackson Pollock. She wore Calder earrings
and didn't like her own nose; an erection could be unscrewed from a statue
when nuns visited the palazzo by the dusty pastel water. She thought Anaïs Nin
very stupid and said "Anaïs Nin was very stupid, wasn't she?"

Floating steps and gravestone for 14 lap dogs, Toro, Pegeen (named dog
                                                                                                   after daughter),
Madame Butterfly, White Angel, Sir Herbert, Hong Kong, all Lhasa because
they are "Zen dogs. They expect kindness and do not bark unless there's a reason,
Peggy who lived in a museum didn't like the murals of Diego Rivera. "Frida Kahlo
is dead," wheelchair and hibiscus, red candles and necklace of miracles.
"One felt how much she must have suffered in this home," turned into museum.

"Rivera, at his death, left no money to his children, who nevertheless adore him.
Instead, he left a fortune to be used to build a monument to himself designed
                                                                                                           by himself."
A woman from Dublin, NH, thought Peggy had done all the paintings
& asked "How do you find the time?" Young women on scholarship as docents
are fashionable sibyls, are from each Allied force. Peggy wore not cat
but bat-butterfly glasses, tinted lagoon, whose sister may have killed
her own children; her father went down with the Titanic.

## Lasso Poem

Lasso poem
                circling words up ahead

                o        o                o

sea horse       *R*

cowboy                gondola,

already in the floating corral
already in the flashing pen.

Lasso poem,
can you toss the dotted line
past the rock formations
of Fig 1 and Fig. 5
—molten wind-chiseled—
past this cursor
bystander?

The Sea Horse tilts
                (really leans into it)
The Cowboy cut-out
tosses the *R*
from a rope poem

parts of the self circling the ascending self

and ropes off

Superman on stilts:

The next time I glance up,
he's several inches closer,
like erratics in a sand garden.

## Troubled Lawns

The felt green lawn seemed to lead up to a monument,
a symbolic house, a bronzed cypress on either side.

We were located on that tense green.
At the other end, a presence we felt but never turned around to see

so we relied on others to tell us what it looked like.
No matter who we really were, we were always agreeing

to be brother and sister, lying on the grass in our tennis whites.
The white farmhouse with sealed doors

the log cabin with a wide and changeless porch
were other weights pinning down the lawn.

\*

The lawn was frequently said to be troubled,
troubled lawns, and dismissed as such

by people with screw-top heads or the shoulders of a bottle.
Oh, those troubled lawns, they said,

and settled back into bullying the albino deck chairs.
Meanwhile, we waited for 2-story high billiard balls to roll over us,

for the round of vectors to be shot off, or the horseman to advance
to avoid the rook and meet the white queen for lunch at that bagel place on Fifth.

"There's been a moratorium on love, the mausoleum to the planetarium
is all lit up, between scribbles and topiaries, the greenhouse is about to collapse,

a rubble of names, in the confusion the plants of moonlight have eaten,"
says a figure to our left, his voice points like a stick,

he speaks like a white flag, his voice on a pole.
We actually said that often about ourselves, that our voice was on a pole

in a vacant, big-building place, like a university during a holiday
or a town in siesta, sunlight a heavy sculpture lying down and dozing

between examples of classical architecture,
whatever we said guarded by a swivel griffin, gold-ball eagle,

raptor of some sort that dropping down as a mustache
lands on the primitive stone head that will appear later in this poem.

But not maybe in a self-piteous way. I'll let "you" be the judge.
Like knick knacks, souvenirs, and carved balls on furniture

one's parents made one live with for years.
Tennis, badminton, lawn games, croquet, alpine skiing, water polo,

we were equipped and knew where to find the folded rules.
Signs had been carved on the inner dome of the ruined observatory,

and they matched the ones scratched in our heads.
We were waiting for the thing at the back of our heads to move.

\*

We talked about the dream we both had of the uncle
showing up with marks of tar on his cheek,

of a massive stone head turning, a sacrificial…
really, a metaphor like commercials for perfume before Christmas.

"There's been a manipulation,"
the voice whispers confidingly, "and someone has left the arboretum in haste,

and the combinations of staircases have fallen into a hole painted black."
The flag sputters. We knew exactly why we were lying

on the grass. Soon a wingéd Victory will appear behind the symbolic house
to touch the corkscrew trees on either side,

and though at first each of our three hearts would light up
and skip out of our chests, playing hopscotch on the touchstones

to the old cemetery, an unpainted house watched us,
and our hearts would be called back. We were flash humans, after all,

permanently imprinted on the grounds, a lawn modified
to be filled only with 4-leaf clover, licked black.

Okay, but I have to be back at the office by 8 on Tuesday.
Here comes the argyle herd of minotaur ready for soccer.

**Deer as Family**


Four deer on a hill. Doe, doe, buck, doe, says
the family at twilight on a walk. It's a family of deer.
Better than boar. Yes, it's better than boredom,
bored (one child just became a teen), formerly, tween at twi-.
See how they browse the light, nibbling. See how we
make use of the last light in the small canvas.
What canvas, they ask, isn't this a poem?
And why small?, quibbling the buds. True, though in
the tunnel of indifference of drainage ancient
and the high collapsible walls, we or they
-cling together like vines-.

# Notes

This book is dedicated to Caroline Knox.

Much love to my husband and daughters, Michael, Sophia, and Simone Miller: you are my beacons. My appreciation also goes to Valeria Losi and her family at their vineyard in Pontignanello, Italy, and to Daniella for her Naples rooftop. I am thankful for the support of James D'Agostino, Mark Drew, Gillian Conoley, Paul Hoover, and Barbara Smith-Mandell. As always, a bow to Laura Mullen, poet and teacher extraordinaire: the writing life and life in general would not be the same without you.

"A Lot of Poems Bathing in a Stream" is a rendition of Wallace Stevens' "A Lot of People Bathing in a Stream."

"How to Become a Writer in 12 Easy Steps" borrows the sentence structure of Michael Earl Craig's first stanza in "Personal Help Library."

"To fill a Gap Insert the Thing that caused it—" contains information from Peggy Guggenheim's *Confessions of an Art Addict* and Anton Gill's *The Art Lover: A Biography of Peggy Guggenheim*. Its title originates with Emily Dickinson.

# Acknowledgements

"Gallery," "Moving Day," and "Venus of Lowell"—*American Journal of Poetry;*
"Table Arrangement"—*Barrow Street;*
"Troubled Lawns"—*Birmingham Poetry Review;*
"Shesangbeyond"—*Bombay Gin;*
"Pellet"—*Boston Review;*
"Edward Hopper Weekend" and "Gusts"—*Chariton Review;*
"Happiest on Earth"—*Cimarron Review;*
"Self-Portrait with Figure in Ski Mask"—*Del Sol Review;*
"'These motorized consorts'"—*Denver Quarterly;*
"Call Number, Postcard, Lava from Pompeii," "Private Writing Gallery," and "On the Flap of an Envelope"—*Diode;*
"Bilingualism" and "Medieval Contemporary American Poetry"—*Forklift, Ohio;*
"Melon"—*The Gettysburg Review;*
"Spiritual Evidence for Life on Earth," "Knick Knack"—*Hotel Amerika;*
"Excellent Bathers"—*LIT;*
"Mixed Border" and "Instant Transmission of Knowledge"—*Map Literary;*
"The water draft," and "Paper Dolls"—*New American Writing;*
"Redux" and "Junk Shop"—*New Delta Review;*
"Open Valley" and "A Lot of Poems Bathing in a Stream"—*North American Review*
"How to Become a Writer in 12 Easy Steps"—*Painted Bride Quarterly;*
"The Real Deal"—*Spoon River Review;*
"Joy, Of, Life" and "Paperweight"—*Volt.*

ALEXANDRIA PEARY is the author of five previous books: *Control Bird Alt Delete, Lid to the Shadow, Fall Foliage Called Bathers & Dancers, Creative Writing Pedagogy for the Twenty-First Century* (with Tom C. Hunley), and *Prolific Moment: Theory and Practice of Mindfulness for Writing*. Her work has received the Iowa Poetry Prize, the Slope Editions Book Prize, and the Joseph Langland Award from the Academy of American Poets. Her poems have been featured at *Poetry Daily* and *Verse Daily* and are listed at the Poetry Foundation: http://www.poetryfoundation.org/bio/alexandria-peary Alexandria's theory of mindful writing is the subject of the blog, http://www.prolificmoment.com/ Her degrees include a MFA from the University of Iowa, a MFA from the University of Massachusetts, Amherst, and a PhD from the University of New Hampshire. She is a professor in the English Department at Salem State University where for eight years she administered the First-Year Writing Program and where she now teaches undergraduate and graduate courses in poetry, nonfiction, fiction, creative writing pedagogy, and mindful writing.

www.ingramcontent.com/pod-product-compliance
Lightning Source LLC
Chambersburg PA
CBHW030101100526
44591CB00008B/221